This doodle book belongs to:

oylan
_____
Your name

2o16
_____
Date

POCKET DOODLES
For Young Artists

BILL ZIMMERMAN
Drawings by Tom Bloom

GIBBS SMITH
TO ENRICH AND INSPIRE HUMANKIND

First Edition
14 13   10 11 12

Text © 2010 Bill Zimmerman
Illustrations © 2010 Tom Bloom

Published by
Gibbs Smith
P.O. Box 667
Layton, Utah 84041

1.800.835.4993 orders
www.gibbs-smith.com

Cover design by Black Eye Design
Interior design by Renee Bond
Manufactured in Manitoba, Canada, in August 2013 by Friesens
Gibbs Smith books are printed on either recycled, 100% post-
consumer waste, FSC-certified papers or on paper produced from
a 100% certified sustainable forest/controlled wood source.

ISBN 13: 978-1-4236-0466-2
ISBN 10: 1-42360-0466-0

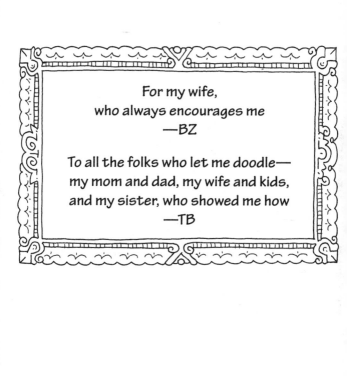

For my wife,
who always encourages me
—BZ

To all the folks who let me doodle—
my mom and dad, my wife and kids,
and my sister, who showed me how
—TB

Dear friend,

Each of us has art within us waiting to come forth. Sometimes we use sticks to make our personal marks in the wet sand; sometimes we use stones to scratch images on cave walls to tell others we were here. Other times, we put crayons and pencil to paper and draw what we see (or want to see). And still other times we make funny, strange-looking doodles while on the phone or in class or at work.

However we do it, art comes from us in many ways. Each of us has a need to express what is inside us, whether in pictures or words or sounds.

This little book encourages you to doodle and draw, color and write, and tap into the artist within you. There are no rules for using this book or for becoming a doodle artist. Anything goes—there are no mistakes in art!

As you turn the pages that follow, choose those that speak to you and spark your imagination. Take your pencil, pen, or crayon, and make the marks and images and words that express what you want to say and who you are. This book will enable you to become the artist of your own world. I hope that you will be thrilled by your rich imagination.

Enjoy!

Sincerely,

Bill Zimmerman

Bill Zimmerman

Create a poster to hang above your bed.

 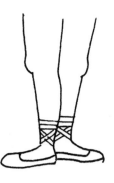

Head to feet . . .

... Make these dancers complete.

Draw a picture of someone you love.

Leonardo da Vinci painted the *Mona Lisa*.
What are they talking about?

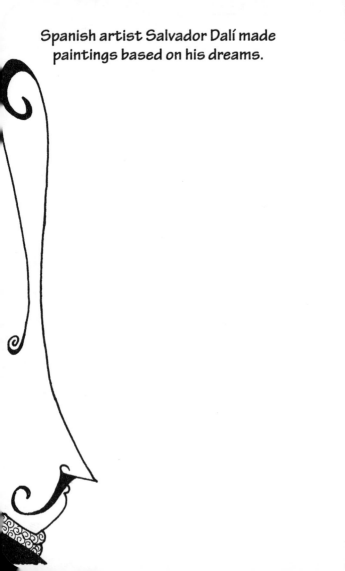

Spanish artist Salvador Dalí made paintings based on his dreams.

Now it's your turn! Draw something
from one of your own dreams.

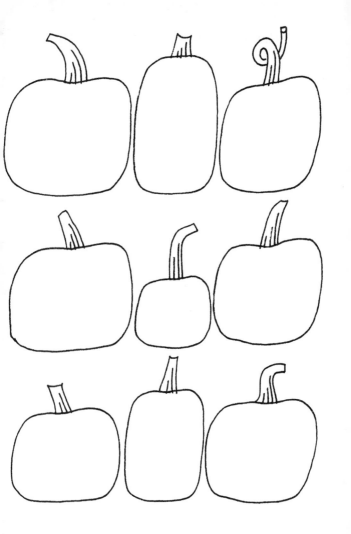

Decorate these pumpkins.

What can you make with these doodles?

Decorate his tee shirt.

What kind of treasure will they find?

Here's a picture.

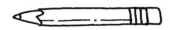

Now you write the story!

What is he lifting?

Can you finish this drawing?

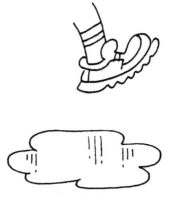

Draw the spider's web.

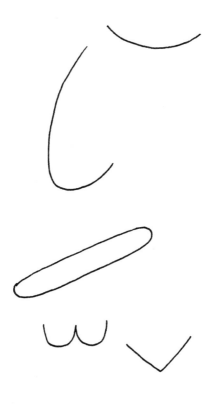

What can you make with these doodles?

Pablo Picasso was a Spanish artist who liked to create inventive portraits. Now it's your turn!

Draw a picture of someone, but try to make it different than usual. Use your imagination!

Can you finish drawing this robot?

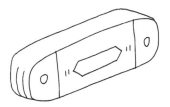

Make a map of an imaginary world.

What's coming out of the piñata?

Finish drawing these faces.

Create a mural for everyone to enjoy.

Give this bird some friends.

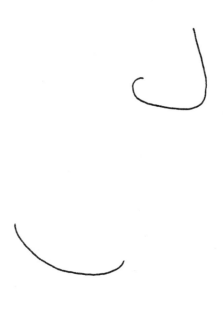

What can you make with these doodles?

Decorate her tee shirt.

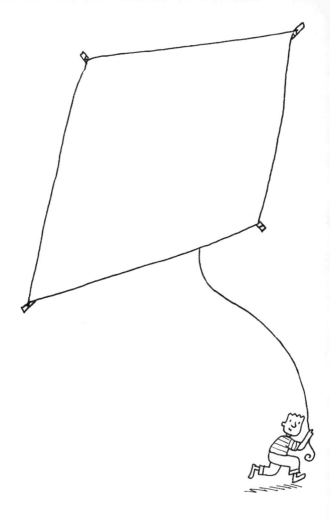

Cover this kite with your artwork.

Landscape . . . What do you see?

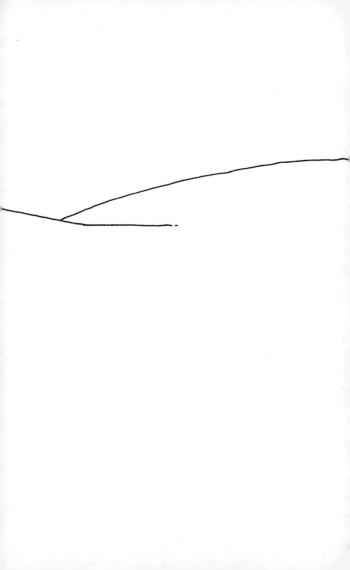

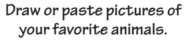

Draw or paste pictures of your favorite animals.

In India, people use the henna plant to paint patterns on their skin. Now it's your turn! Decorate her arm and hand with your own henna design.

What is she saying?

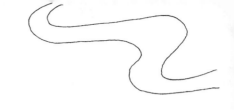

What do they find underwater?

Can you finish building the Eiffel Tower?

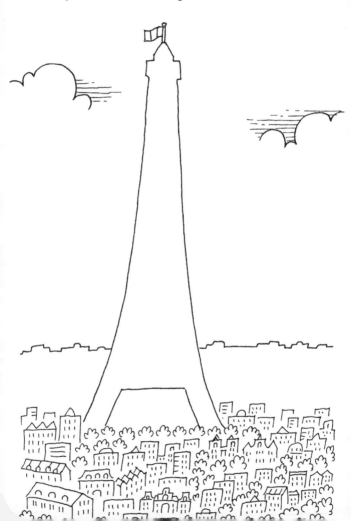

Dutch artist Vincent van Gogh liked to paint pictures of sunflowers. Add some sunflowers to this vase.

You live under the sea?!

What are they saying?

Draw a happy memory.

Give her a beautiful headdress to wear.

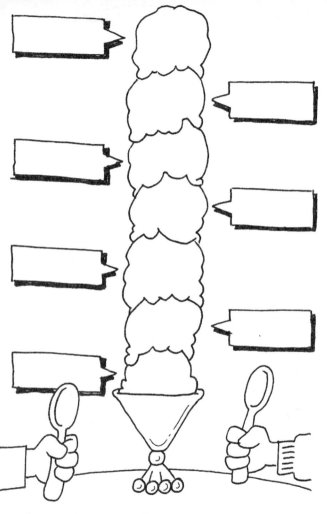

Invent some new flavors of ice cream.

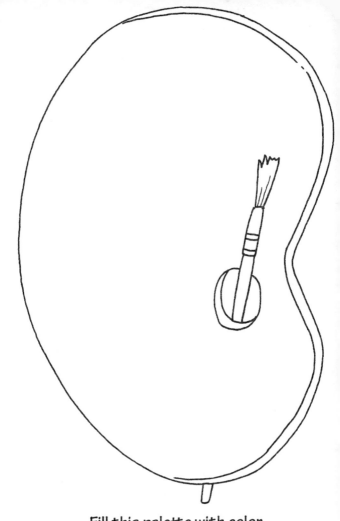

Fill this palette with color.

Can you finish this drawing?

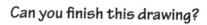

Color this page and add something new.

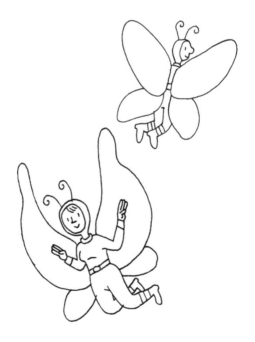

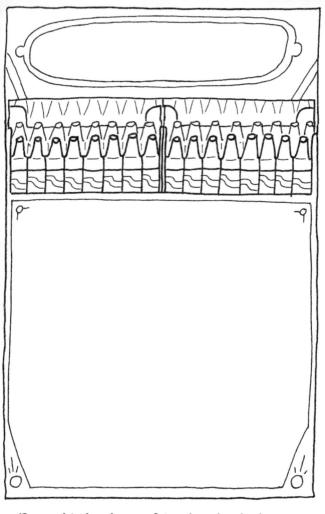

Pass this book to a friend and ask them
to draw something on this page.

Something has landed on his head!

Draw a creature with the body of
a lion, the head of a dragon,

the wings of an eagle, and the tail of a serpent. Oh, and it breathes fire, too!

Decorate this Japanese screen.

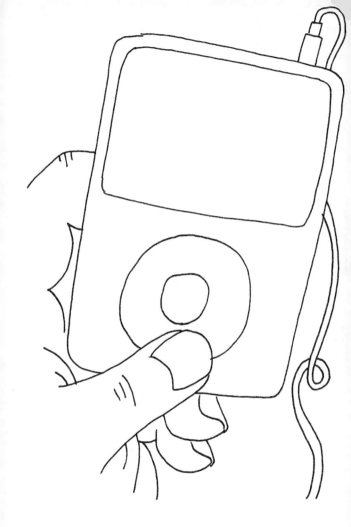

What are you listening to?

Help decorate this pottery.

What's growing in this field?

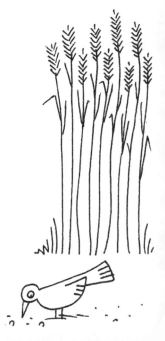

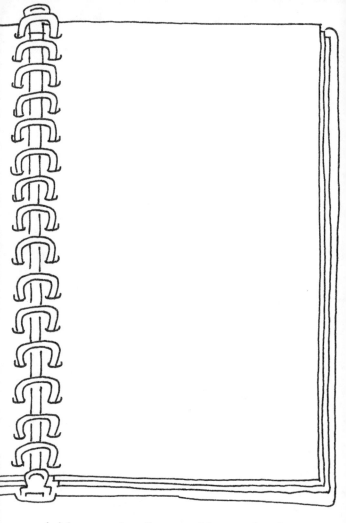

Add some doodles to this notebook.

What do they discover in the rain forest?

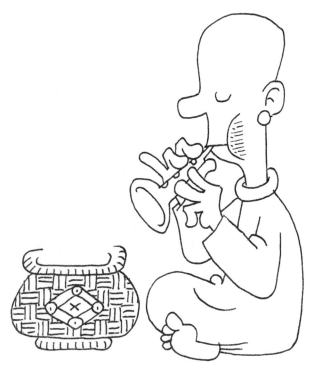

What is coming out of the basket?

The circus is in town! Create a poster.

What is he singing?

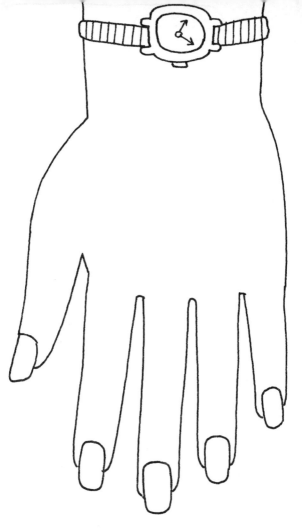

Decorate her fingernails.

French artist Henri Matisse liked to cut out paper shapes and glue them together to create a form of art called a collage.

Now it's your turn! Cut out paper
shapes from a magazine and paste them
here to create your own collage.

What is he dreaming about?

Can you finish this drawing?

What can you make with these doodles?

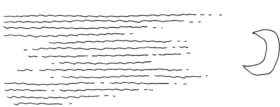

What's on top of this building?

Give each of these people a hat to wear.

What are they thinking about?

Here's a picture.

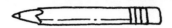

Now you write the story!

Add a new building to the city.

Decorate her tee shirt.

What kind of dog is he walking?

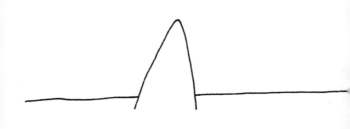

Can you finish this drawing?

Help Michelangelo paint scenes
on your bedroom ceiling.

Add some drawings to these ancient stones.

Draw the person wearing these clothes.

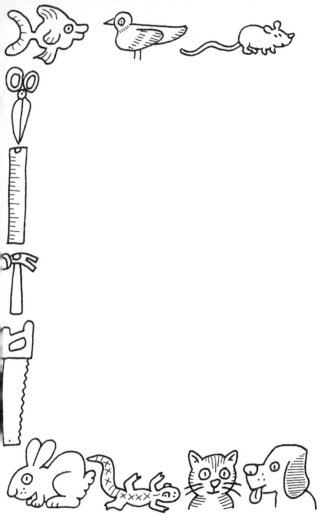

Design a house for your pet.

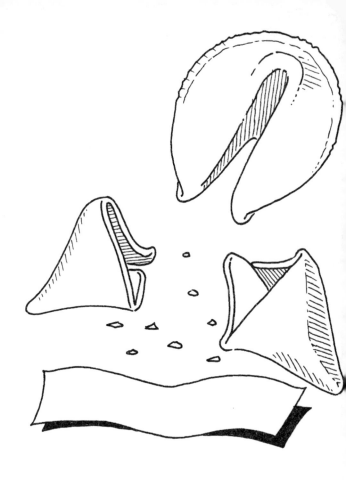

Write a fortune you'd like to read.

Add some sculptures or statues to this park.

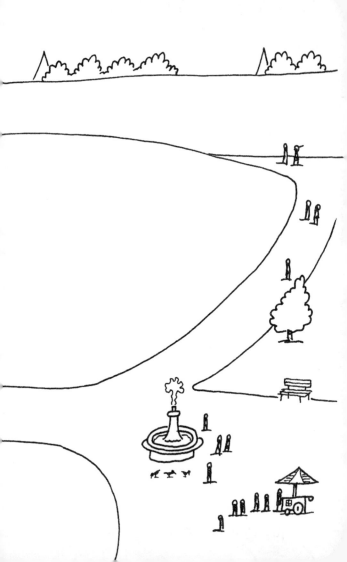

Design the ticket and musical program for tonight's concert.

What's the next step?

Finish drawing these faces.

Create a new wonder for the world.

Where is the bumblebee going?

Give this dog a head.

Can you finish drawing these cars?

Who's there?

Draw your favorite superhero.

It's the Fourth of July!

Draw fireworks in the sky.

Design a flag for these pirates.

What can you make with these doodles?

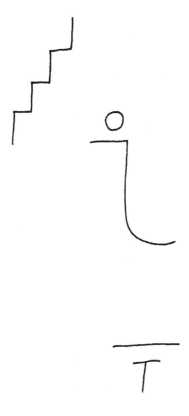

What are they looking at?

Can you finish this drawing?

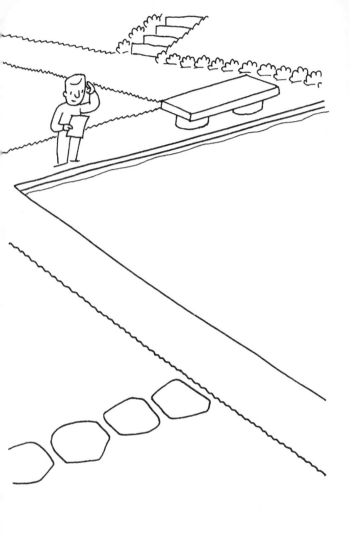

What does he see in the pool?

Decorate this kimono.

Here's a picture.

Now you write the story!

What do you see outside the window?

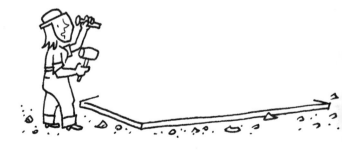

What is she making?

Decorate the bird's tee shirt.

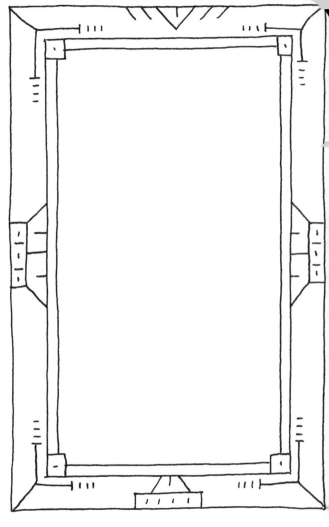

Draw something funny.

There goes Bigfoot!

Draw a picture of your best friend.

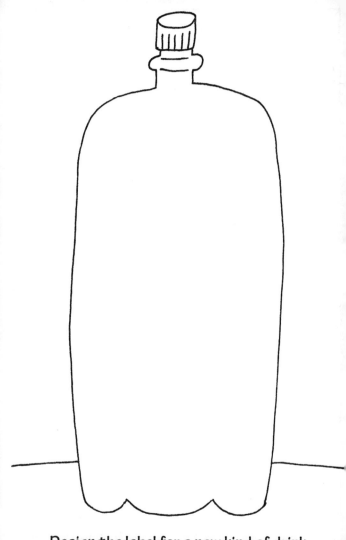

Design the label for a new kind of drink.

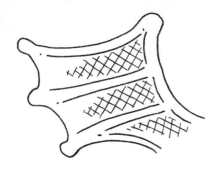

Draw the creatures that go with these wings.

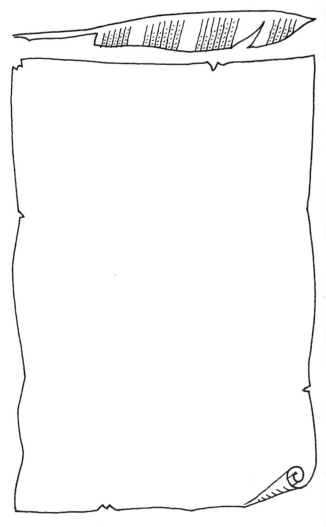

Practice writing your signature on this page.

Draw some butterflies for her to catch.

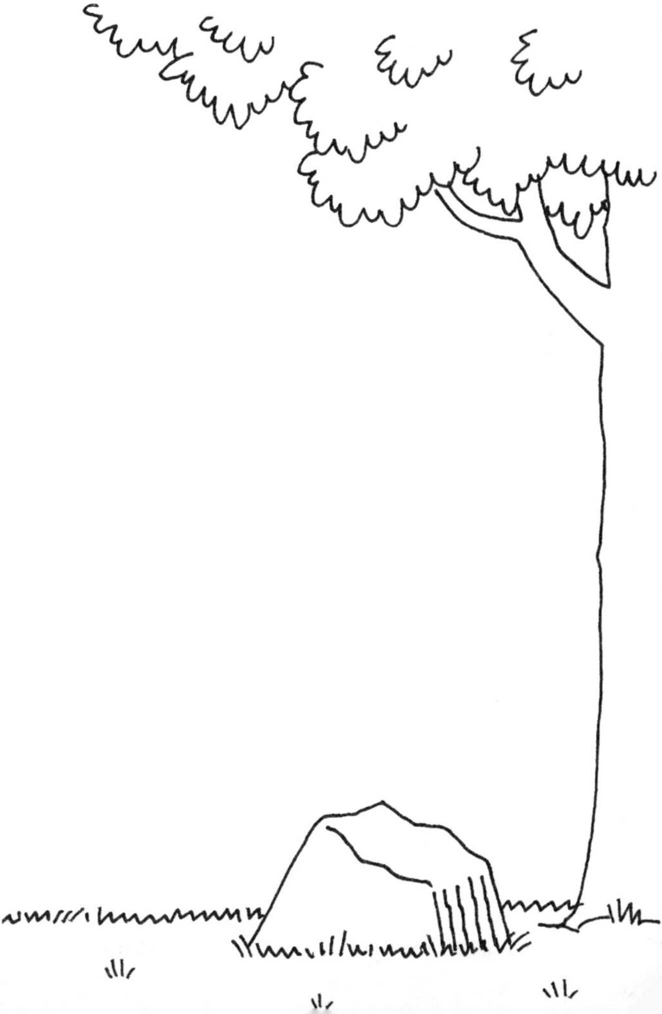

Give these people some sunglasses.

Draw some flowers blooming from this cactus.

Decorate this airship.

What is he lifting?

Decorate the welcome mat for this house.

What are they saying?

Georgia O'Keeffe was famous for painting detailed images of flowers.

Now it's your turn! Look closely at a
flower and then draw what you see.

Make a drawing that includes one or more
of the objects shown on this page.

Can you finish this drawing?

Finish drawing these people.

Draw something that happened to you today.
It can be happy or sad.

Can you finish this drawing?

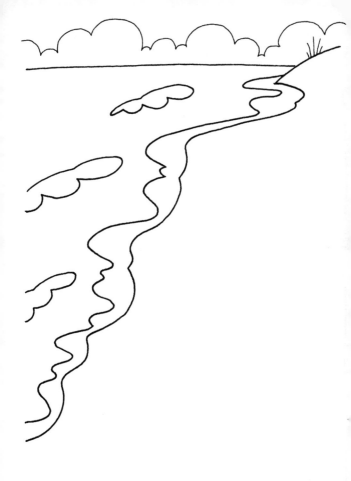

What do you see at the beach?

On these scrolls, draw some memorable
events from your life so far.

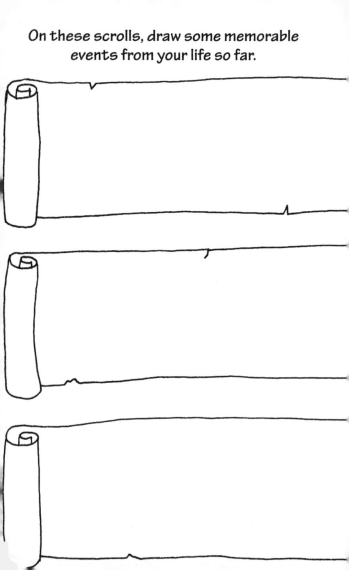

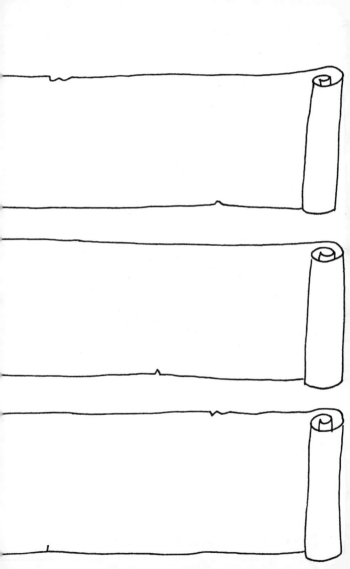

Color this page and add something new.

Give this guy a new hairdo.

A ninja is battling a berserk robot!

What are they saying?

Sea monster, ahoy!

Draw someone you think is cute or handsome.

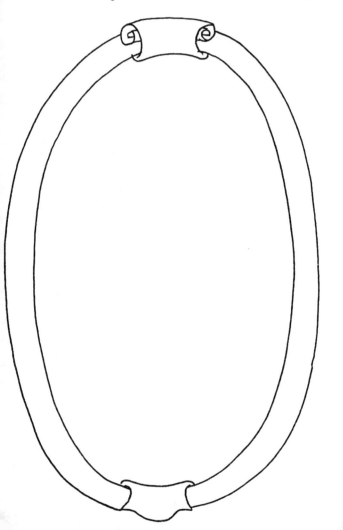

Decorate this Christmas tree.

Make a new ride for the amusement park.

Can you finish this drawing?

Here's a picture.

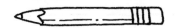

Now you write the story!

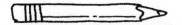

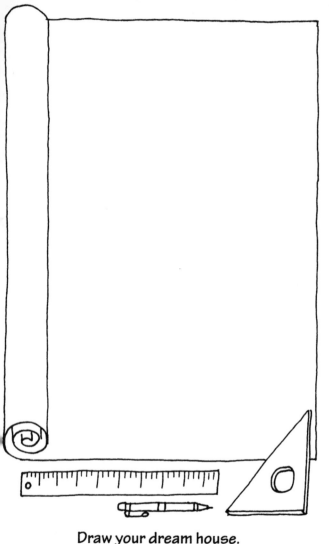

Draw your dream house.

Decorate the alligator's tee shirt.

Can you finish this drawing?

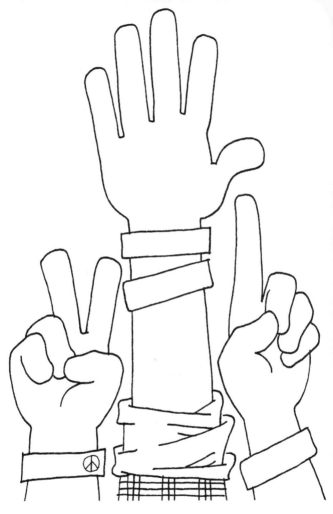

Write some of your favorite
words on these wristbands.

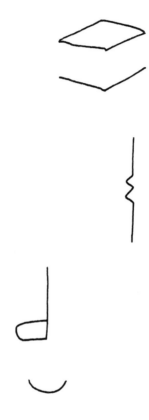

What can you make with these doodles?

Create some signs for this busy street.

Can you finish building this bridge?

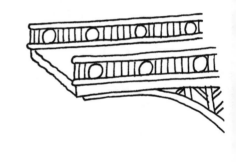

What can you make with these doodles?

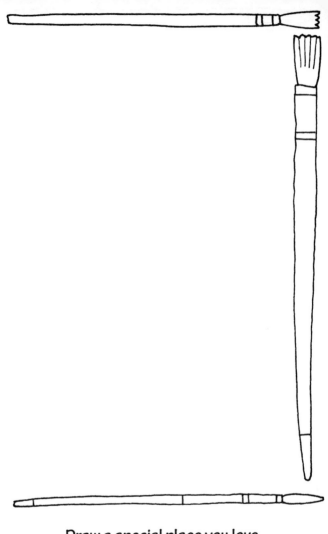

Draw a special place you love.

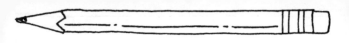

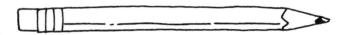

Use this page to invent some new words.

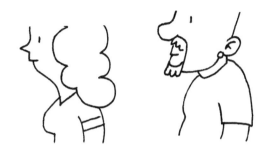

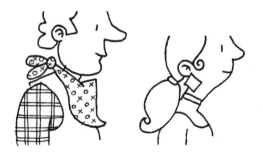

Give each of these people a hat to wear.

French artist Georges Seurat painted
pictures with dots instead of lines or strokes.

Now it's your turn! Try making your own picture using only dots.

Write messages on these candy hearts.

Decorate this beach towel.

What is she climbing?

What are they saying?

Create a statue for the park.

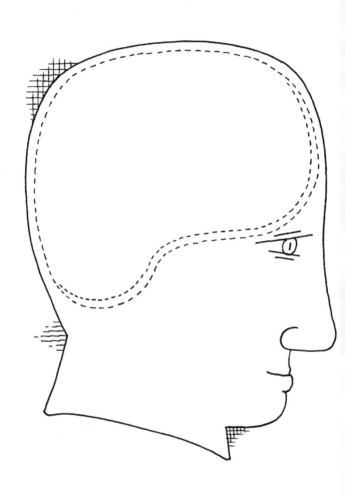

What is this artist thinking about?

Draw a unicorn for this tapestry.

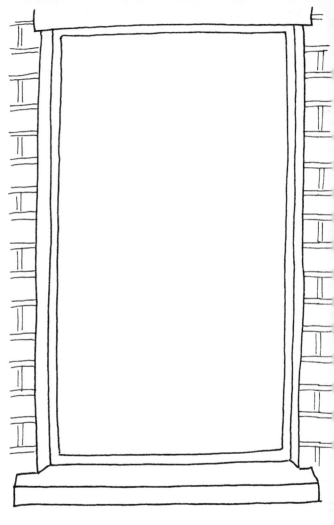

What do you see through the window?

What do you see in the sky?

Decorate this snowboard.

Can you finish this drawing?

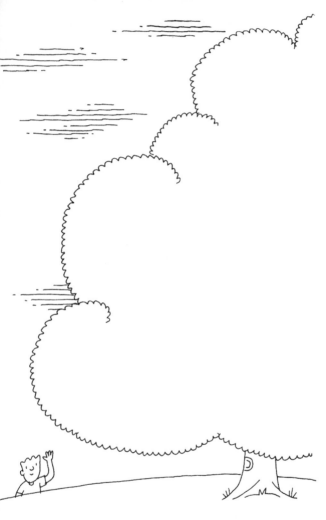

Fill this tree with birds and animals.

Decorate her tee shirt.

What are they watching on the movie screen?

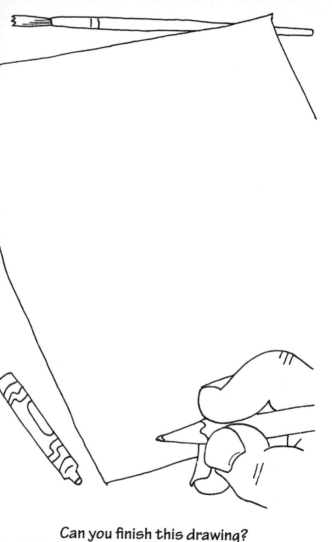

Can you finish this drawing?

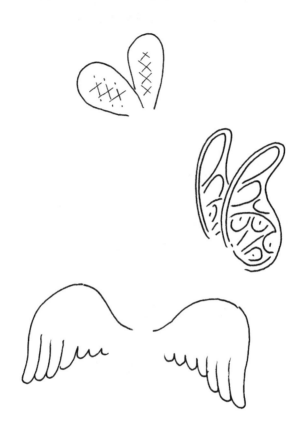

Draw the creatures that go with these wings.

What trick is the clown performing?

Design your own cereal box.

It's raining cats and dogs!

It's raining bats and frogs!

Draw your favorite dinosaur.

Can you finish this drawing?

A coat of arms shows what's important
to you and your family. In the space
above, create your own coat of arms!

What is he drawing on the wall?

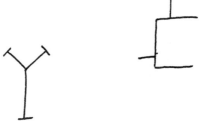

What can you make with these doodles?

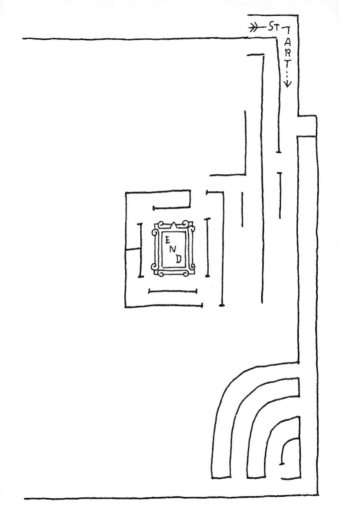

Can you finish this maze?

Snowball fight!

Draw a reflection in the water.

What are they singing about?

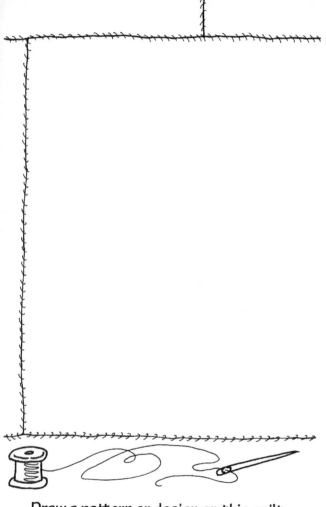

Draw a pattern or design on this quilt.

Give these fairies some wings to fly.

What is making these tracks?

What kind of dog is he walking?

Decorate this teepee.

Free space—draw anything you want!

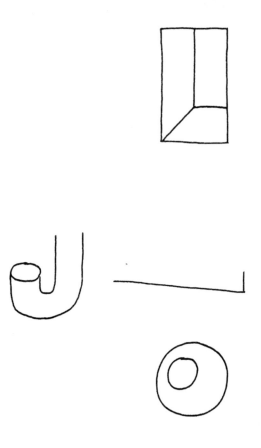

What can you make with these doodles?

Seascape . . . What do you see?

Color this page and add something new.

Create a statue for the town square.

What is he looking at?

Finish drawing these people.

Can you finish this city?

Add buildings, houses, people,
and anything else you want!

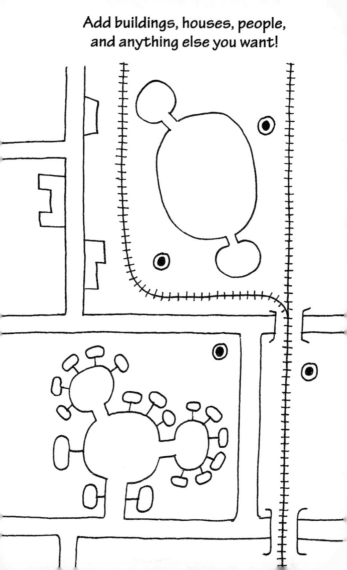

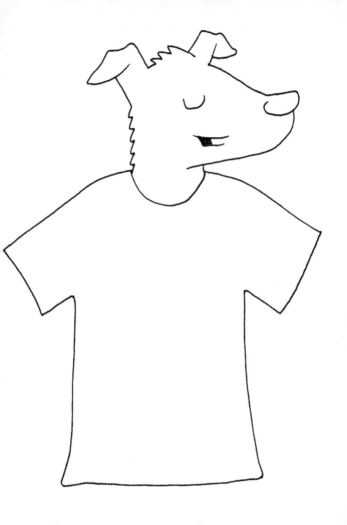

Decorate the dog's tee shirt.

Draw something that has bright lights.

Here's a picture.

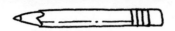

Now you tell the story!

Design a rug for this room.

What are they saying?

Decorate the Statue of Liberty
for the Fourth of July.

Decorate the Statue of Liberty
for Christmas.

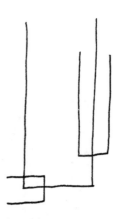

What can you make with these doodles?

Decorate her tee shirt.

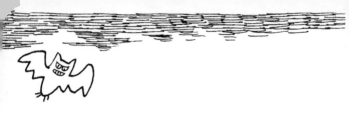

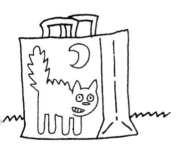

It's Halloween!

Draw everyone wearing their costumes.

Decorate this page with your favorite colors.

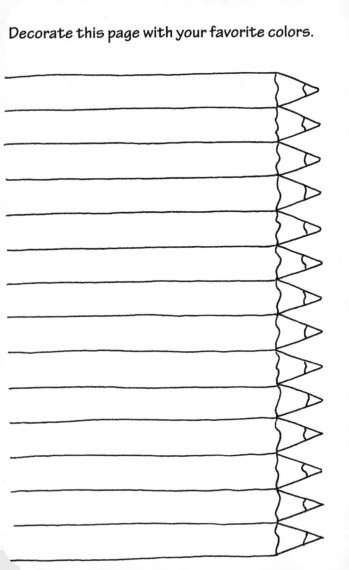

Can you finish this drawing?

Draw the designs his skates
have made in the ice.

Draw something to go on top of this building.

Give her a new hat to wear.

Here's a picture.

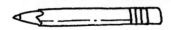

Now you tell the story!

Design this plate.

The show is about to start!
Finish drawing the clown.

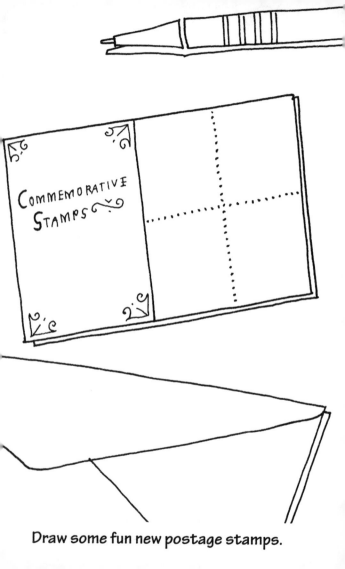

COMMEMORATIVE STAMPS

Draw some fun new postage stamps.

Add something new and color this page.

American artist Alexander Calder created
a miniature circus from wire, string,
rubber, cloth, and other objects.

Now it's your turn! Draw your own miniature circus here.

She has just finished making a giant
cake. What does it look like?

What are you taking a picture of?

Who's in the spotlight?

Help! He needs a parachute. Or does he?

Create some mosaic-tile
artwork to go on this wall.

What's everybody looking at?

Draw something that looks weird.

What have they discovered?

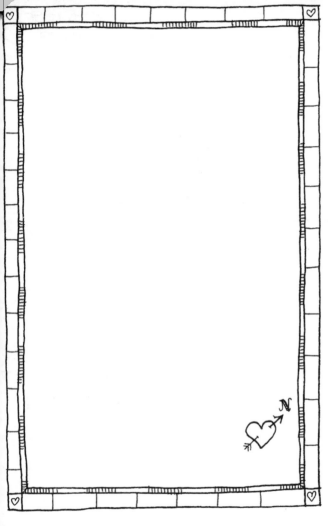

Draw a picture of something you love.

Can you finish drawing the mermaid?

**What ideas are floating around
in this artist's head?**

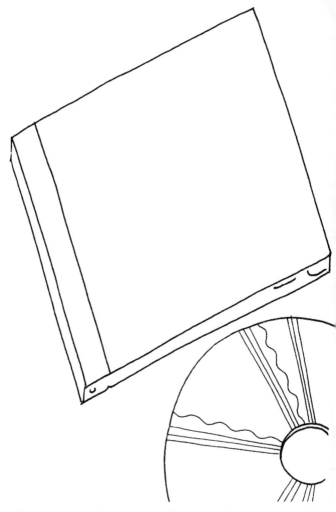

Create an album cover for your favorite music.

What has she painted on her canvas?

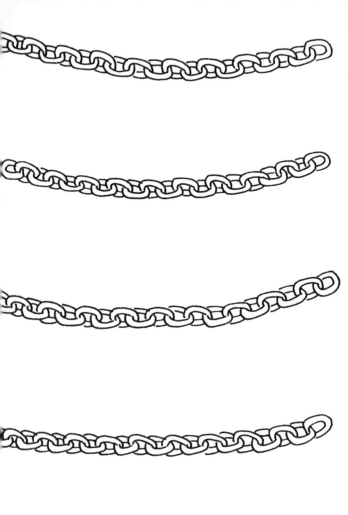

Add your favorite charms or
jewelry to these bracelets.

Draw or paste pictures of
your family or friends.

Add some flowers to this vase.

What do these signs say?

Here's a picture.

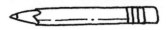

Now you tell the story!

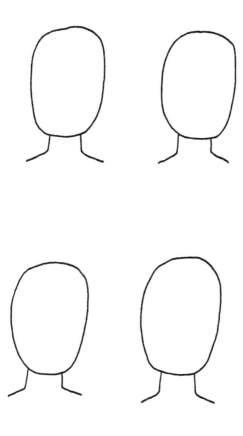

Finish drawing these faces.

What are they saying?

He came out of a manhole and found a
different world. What does it look like?

Draw your favorite animal.

Draw the people wearing these hats.

Decorate her tee shirt.

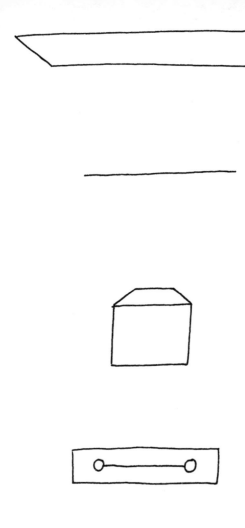

What can you make with these doodles?

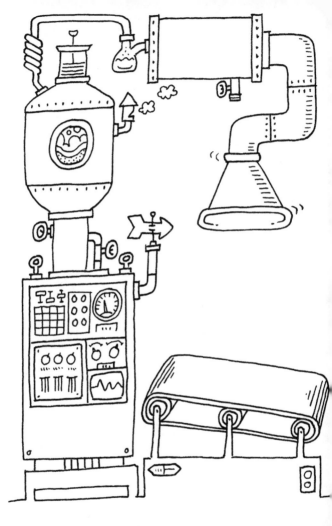

What is coming out of this machine?

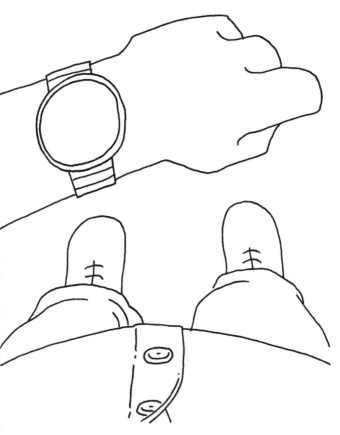

You just got a cool new watch.
What does it do?

Can you finish this drawing?

About Bill Zimmerman

Bill Zimmerman has made it his life's work to pioneer interactive techniques that help people tap into their creativity and express themselves through writing and drawing. He has authored seventeen other books, including *Pocketdoodles for Kids*; *Doodles and Daydeams: Your Passport for Becoming an Escape Artist*; and *Your Life in Comics: 100 Things for Guys to Write and Draw*.

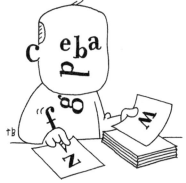

Visit Bill's Web sites:
www.makebeliefscomix.com
www.billztreasurechest.com

About Tom Bloom

Tom Bloom is a dandy doodler. His doodles have been published in *The New York Times*, *The Wall Street Journal*, *The New Yorker*, *Games*, and *Nickelodeon*. His family lives in New York. He lives in his imagination.

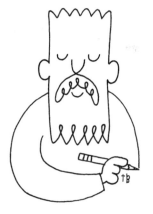

Share With Us!

We welcome your feedback on this book. What do you like to draw? Please send us your suggestions on how we can improve this book, along with your permission to use your ideas in future printings. For every idea used, a free copy of *Pocketdoodles for Young Artists* will be sent to you.

Send your comments to:
Bill Zimmerman
MakeBeliefsComix.com
201 West 77 Street, Suite 6A
New York, NY 10024
billz@makebeliefscomix.com

Also by Bill Zimmerman and Tom Bloom

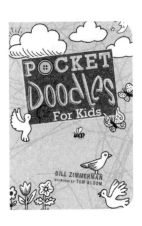